A Complete Guide to Wilderness Survival

Outdoor Fun Made Easy: Learn How to Build Shelters, Start fires, and Explore Nature

By A. Cox

DEDICATION:

To my dad, who instilled a love of the outdoors in me since I could walk. Thank you for all of the tidepools explored, the camping trips taken, and the rivers rafted.

Dear Reader,

Thank you so much for reading my book! As a special thank you for reading my book, scan the QR code below to get your free Nature Detective's Handbook, a fun activity book that includes over 50 pages of activities for your child to explore more of the outdoors! Designed especially for the US state parks!

Copyright © 2024 by A. Cox

All rights reserved. No portion of this book may be reproduced in any form without written permission from the publisher or author, except as permitted by U.S. copyright law.

Table of Contents

Introduction 9
   Why Should You Learn Survival Skills? 9
   What Wonders Await You? 9
   It's All About Having Fun and Learning! 10

Chapter 1: Pack Up, Gear Up: How to Prepare for Any Adventure 11
   Introduction to Outdoor Survival 11
      Importance of being prepared 11
      Basic safety rules for outdoor activities 12
      Fast Facts 13
      Life Savers 13
   Essential Gear and Packing Tips for Young Explorers 13
      Packing your survival kit: What's inside? 13
      Choosing the right adventure outfit and shoes 14
      Must-have tools and supplies for young explorers 14
      Did You Know? 15
   Understanding Your Environment 15
      Types of natural environments: what to watch out for 16
      Weather patterns and their impacts 16
   Planning Your Adventure 17
      Set goals and limits 17
      Learn to use a map 17
      Tell someone about your plan 17
      Life Savers 18
   Fun Activity: Pack Your Backpack 18
      Instructions 18
   Quiz: True or False 19
   Interactive Quiz: Are You Ready to Explore? 19

Chapter 2: Trail Tricks: Finding Your Way and Making Camp 21
   Natural Navigation Techniques 21
      Using the sun 21
      Star navigation 21
      Landmarks 22

- Shadow stick method 22
- Observing nature 22
- Did You Know? 22
- Finding and Creating Shelter 22
  - Types of natural shelters 23
  - Materials used for making shelters 23
  - Step-by-step guide to building a basic lean-to shelter 23
  - Fast Facts 24
- Safe Shelter Practices 24
  - Choosing a safe spot 24
  - Importance of staying warm and dry 24
- Fun Activity: Build Your Virtual Shelter 25
- Quiz: Can You Navigate and Build Like a Pro? 26

Chapter 3: Meet the Forest Friends: How to Watch Wildlife Safely 27
- Understanding Wildlife 27
  - Animals you might see 27
  - Animal behaviours and signs 28
  - Fast Facts 28
- Safety Measures and Precautions 28
  - Do's and don'ts when you see wild animals 28
  - How to keep your campsite safe from wildlife 29
- What to Do If... Scenarios 29
  - If you bump into a snake on your path 29
  - If you see a bear 29
  - If bees start buzzing around you 30
  - If you get lost 30
  - Life Savers 30
  - Did You Know? 30
- Respect for Nature 30
  - Why we should not disturb wildlife 31
  - Leave No Trace principles 32
- Interactive Activity: Wildlife Safety Quiz 31

Chapter 4: Be a Wilderness Doctor: First Aid Fun 33
- Basic First Aid Skills 33

Treating your cuts, scrapes, and bruises	33
Insect bites and stings	34
Fast Facts	34
Handling Serious Emergencies	35
What to do if you think you have hypothermia?	35
Staying Healthy Outdoors	36
Hydration is key	36
Eating right in the wild	36
Keeping Clean	37
Interactive Activity: First Aid Simulation	37
Activity setup	38
How it works	38
Learning objectives	38
Staying Healthy and Happy	39
Avoiding bug bites	39
Safe eating practices	39
What to do if you think you ate something bad?	40
Quiz: First Aid and Staying Healthy Outdoors	40
Chapter 5: Crafty in the Wild: Making Tools and Fire	**43**
Foraging Fun: Finding Food in Nature	43
Safe plants and insects to eat	43
Learning to harvest: how to be a nature-friendly forager	44
Beware of look-alikes	44
Fast Facts	45
The Basics of Hunting and Fishing	45
Simple traps for small animals	45
Fishing is fun with just a few things!	46
Ethical hunting and fishing: caring for nature	46
Did You Know?	47
Adventure Crafting in the Woods: Become a Nature Detective and Inventor!	48
Fun simple tools to make	48
Safety Tips	49
Interactive Activity: Create Your Survival Tool	49
What you'll need	49

 How to make your survival tool?...49

 What you'll learn..50

Fire-Making Techniques...50

 Safety first while handling fire..51

Quiz: Important Survival Techniques..52

Final Words..54

Wilderness Whiz: The Answer Key to Your Outdoor Quizzes 57

Chapter 1..57

Chapter 2..57

Chapter 3..58

Chapter 4..58

Chapter 5..58

INTRODUCTION

Hey, kid. Are you ready to become a wilderness explorer?

If you said "yes!" out loud, then you're in luck!

This book is your secret map to learning how to be safe, have fun, and take care of yourself while adventuring in the great outdoors.

WHY SHOULD YOU LEARN SURVIVAL SKILLS?

Picture this: You're an explorer in the big, green forest. You're using sticks and leaves to build your very own campsite. Along your journey, you discover secret spots where clean, sparkling water flows. And if you ever need to call for help, you use only the things around you in nature to send signals. What an adventure!

When you learn survival skills, you can have safe adventures and become a hero of the wild.

That's what you'll pick up in this survival guide. You'll learn how to be smart, safe, and super cool – all while taking good care of Mother Nature.

WHAT WONDERS AWAIT YOU?

Here's a sneak peek of the adventures you'll go on through each chapter:

- *"Pack Up, Gear Up: How to Prepare for Any Adventure"* – This chapter teaches you how to pack your adventure bag, pick the right tools, and plan your trip like a real explorer.
- *"Trail Tricks: Finding Your Way and Making Camp"* – Learn how to use the stars and trees to find your way and build a snug shelter to curl up in at night.
- *"Meet the Forest Friends: How to Watch Wildlife Safely"* – Discover the animals of the forest and learn how to watch them without getting too close. It's all about keeping you and the animals safe and happy.
- *"Be a Wilderness Doctor: First Aid Fun"* – Oops! Got a scrape or a bug bite? No worries! This chapter will show you how to fix it up and keep exploring.
- *"Crafty in the Wild: Making Tools and Fire"* – Ever wanted to make your own tools like a real survival expert? Learn how to use what nature gives you to make things like a fire without matches and even cool tools from branches and stones.

IT'S ALL ABOUT HAVING FUN AND LEARNING!

Each chapter has puzzles, easy-to-follow instructions for fun activities, and awesome facts to help you see just what to do. You'll learn loads, have heaps of fun, and get ready to handle your own adventures.

So, what are you waiting for?

Grab your sense of adventure, and let's go into the wild!

Chapter 1:

PACK UP, GEAR UP: HOW TO PREPARE FOR ANY ADVENTURE

Whether you're exploring a deep, green forest, climbing up a rocky mountain, or trekking across a big, sandy desert, being prepared is super important. This chapter is like your treasure map for getting ready, knowing all about where you're going, and planning your exciting trip.

Let's start this journey with the right foot forward!

INTRODUCTION TO OUTDOOR SURVIVAL

Going into the wilderness is like stepping into a whole new world – a place where *nature* makes the rules, and not your parents. To have fun and stay safe out there, it's really important to know some basic outdoor survival tricks. This part of the book will show you why it's cool to be prepared, teach you some important safety rules, and give you smart tips to handle surprises along the way.

IMPORTANCE OF BEING PREPARED

Getting ready the right way is like putting on superhero armor – it helps protect you from any trouble you might run into. It means not just stuffing your backpack with cool gadgets, but also thinking about what could happen out there. When you plan ahead, you can dodge dangers and be super quick at solving problems if they pop up from the bushes!

BASIC SAFETY RULES FOR OUTDOOR ACTIVITIES

When you're out exploring nature, staying safe is super important.

Here are some cool rules to follow so you can enjoy your wild adventure without any worries:

- *Pack the Right Stuff:* Even if it's just a short hike, always pack the most important things.
- *Check the Weather:* Always know the weather before and during your adventure. It's important to be prepared for any changes.
- *Learn About the Trail:* Know as much as you can about where you're going. Check the trail conditions. Know when it gets dark and if there are any streams you'll cross.
- *Stay on Marked Trails:* This helps you not get lost and keeps all the plants and animals safe.
- *Use the Buddy System:* Always have a friend with you. It's more fun and you can look out for each other.
- *Tell Someone Your Plans:* Before you go hiking, let someone know where you're going and when you expect to be back. This way, someone will know where to find you if you're late.
- *Extra Safety Gear:* Think about bringing a whistle and a personal locator beacon. These can help others find you if you need help.
- *Know When to Turn Back:* If you feel unsure or unsafe, it's okay to turn back. The trail will still be there another day.
- *Stay Calm if Things Go Wrong:* If something unexpected happens, stay calm. This will help you think clearly and use your gear and knowledge to stay safe.

FAST FACTS

Every year, lots of people are rescued because they were ready and knew important survival tips. Did you know? If you know how to use mirrors or make loud sounds to call for help, you can be found much faster!

LIFE SAVERS

Always carry a whistle – it can be heard from far away! Also, a signal mirror is super useful because it works even when it's cloudy. These tools can really help rescuers find you quickly if you ever need help.

ESSENTIAL GEAR AND PACKING TIPS FOR YOUNG EXPLORERS

PACKING YOUR SURVIVAL KIT: WHAT'S INSIDE?

When you go on an adventure outdoors, having the right gear makes it not only safer but way more fun! This part of the book will help you understand what you should pack in your survival kit, how to choose clothes that are just right for the outdoors, and pick tools that are super important if you ever need help!

Your survival kit is like a treasure chest for adventure – it holds everything you need to take care of yourself in the wild!

Let's see what magical items should be in your kit:

- *Water and Hydration:* Always bring a tough water bottle. Don't forget water purification tablets or a little water filter. Staying hydrated is key to staying strong and healthy on your journey.
- *Food:* Pack snacks that give you lots of energy but don't spoil, like nuts, jerky, and energy bars. They're like fuel for your adventure engine!

- *First Aid Kit:* This is your healing box. It should have bandages, antiseptic wipes for cleaning cuts, tape, pain relievers, allergy meds, and any other medicines you need.
- *Emergency Shelter:* Carry something light like an emergency tent or a space blanket to keep you safe from wind, rain, and cold.
- *Fire Starting Gear:* Waterproof matches, a lighter, and something to help catch fire (like tinder) are important for making a fire. This keeps you warm and lets you cook yummy campfire food!

CHOOSING THE RIGHT ADVENTURE OUTFIT AND SHOES

When you're planning to explore the great outdoors, wearing the right clothes and shoes is super important! It's like dressing up for a weather adventure.

HERE'S HOW YOU CAN LAYER UP:

- *Base Layer:* Start with clothes that keep you dry. Look for materials that can pull sweat away from your skin.
- *Insulating Layer:* Next, wear something cozy like wool or fleece to keep you warm.
- *Outer Layer:* Top it off with a jacket that's both waterproof and breathable. This layer is your shield against rain, wind, and cold.
- *Shoes*: Your shoes should be tough, comfy, and right for where you're walking. Like boots for a rocky hike or lighter shoes for a trail.

MUST-HAVE TOOLS AND SUPPLIES FOR YOUNG EXPLORERS

Besides the usual stuff in your pack, there are a few cool tools that can make your adventure safer and more fun:

- *Multi-tool or Swiss Army Knife:* These are like a toolbox you can fit in your pocket! They have all sorts of gadgets like a knife, pliers, and even a screwdriver, helping you fix things or get creative in the wild.
- *Flashlight or Headlamp:* Having a light with you is a must, especially if it gets dark while you're still outside. Don't forget to bring some extra batteries just in case.
- *Navigation Tools:* Always carry a map and a compass. They're your best friends for finding your way around, even better if you also have a GPS. But remember, gadgets can run out of power, so knowing how to use a map and compass is super cool!

UNDERSTANDING YOUR ENVIRONMENT

When you're planning an outdoor adventure, knowing about the place you're going to explore is super important for staying safe and having fun. Every different place, like forests, mountains, or deserts, has its own challenges and cool things to know.

> *Did You Know?*
> The Swiss Army Knife is a really cool tool that was made way back in the 1890s. It was first designed to help soldiers in the Swiss army do important things like take apart their rifles and open cans of food. Imagine having a tool that could do all that!

TYPES OF NATURAL ENVIRONMENTS: WHAT TO WATCH OUT FOR

- *Forests:* Forests are full of trees and plants, which can make it hard to see far and tricky to find your way. Be careful of things like branches that might fall or bumpy paths that could trip you up.
- *Mountains:* Being up high in the mountains can make you feel different because of the thin air. The weather can change really quickly too, and you might meet some wild animals. Always stay prepared!
- *Deserts:* Deserts don't have much water, and the weather can get super hot in the day and really cold at night. Remember to wear sunscreen and a hat to protect yourself from the sun.

WEATHER PATTERNS AND THEIR IMPACTS

The weather can change your outdoor plans a lot! It's smart to understand what the weather might do before you go:

- *Reading Clouds and Wind:* If you can look at the clouds and feel the wind, you might be able to tell if a storm is coming. This can help you decide if it's safe to keep going or better to head back.
- *Knowing Seasonal Weather:* Each part of the year can have different weather, like rain in the spring or heat in the summer. Knowing this can help you pack and plan better.

If You…get caught by surprise by bad weather, the first thing you should do is find a place to stay dry and warm. It's really important to keep your body cozy to stop from getting too cold, which can make you sick. Always bring things like a light tarp or a space blanket with you just in case you need to make a quick shelter.

PLANNING YOUR ADVENTURE

Before you start your outdoor adventure, it's important to have a good plan to make sure you have lots of fun and stay safe!

Here's how you can make a great plan for your adventure:

SET GOALS AND LIMITS

First, think about what you want to do on your adventure. Maybe you want to get to the top of a hill, learn how to start a camp fire, or just enjoy the trees and birds. Knowing what you want to do helps you get ready and stay safe.

LEARN TO USE A MAP

Knowing how to look at maps is super important:

- Maps help you see what the land looks like, like where the hills and valleys are.
- Choose a path that's just right for your adventure level and what you want to see. And have a backup plan, just in case you need to change your path if something unexpected happens.

TELL SOMEONE ABOUT YOUR PLAN

Always share your plan with someone who isn't going with you:

- Tell them where you're going.
- Tell them when you think you'll be back.
- Give them a way to contact you.
- Let them know what they should do if you don't come back on time.

LIFE SAVERS

If something goes wrong, knowing how to call for help and who to call can be a lifesaver. Make sure you and your friends know what to do in an emergency before you start your adventure.

FUN ACTIVITY: PACK YOUR BACKPACK

Now that you know how to get ready, let's put that knowledge to use. This activity will help you think about what you should take with you for a day of fun in the wild.

INSTRUCTIONS:

Here's a list of things you might need. Choose which ones you'd put in your backpack for a day trip. Think about where you'll be and what challenges you might face.

- Checklist:

☐ Map
☐ Compass
☐ Waterbottle
☐ Snacks(nuts, jerky, energy bars)
☐ Raincoat
☐ Flashlight
☐ Multi-tool
☐ Firstaidkit
☐ Sunscreen
☐ Hat
☐ Emergency whistle

QUIZ: TRUE OR FALSE

1. "You should bring a large, heavy tent for every outdoor trip."
2. "It's necessary to carry a way to clean water even on short trips."

INTERACTIVE QUIZ: ARE YOU READY TO EXPLORE?

Question 1: What should you always tell someone before you go on an adventure?

    A. Your plans and where you're going

    B. Your favourite colour

    C. What you packed for lunch

Question 2: Which of these items should you include in your survival kit?

    A. Your favourite toy

    B. A flashlight and extra batteries

    C. A pillow

Question 3: Why is it important to pack layers of clothing when going on an adventure?

    A. Layers help you stay comfy and safe as the weather changes

    B. You can change your outfit if you get bored

    C. They make you look cool

Question 4: What is a good way to make sure you don't get lost?

    A. Follow the animals

    B. Carry a map and a compass

    C. Just guess which way to go

This activity helps you remember what you've learned and makes you think about what you really need to be safe and comfy on your adventures. When you pack your backpack smartly, you're ready for surprises and can have lots of fun on your journey.

Chapter 2:

TRAIL TRICKS: FINDING YOUR WAY AND MAKING CAMP

Learning how to find your way through nature and building a simple shelter are super important skills for any young explorer like you. This chapter will show you how to find your way through nature using only what's around you and how to build a cozy shelter to keep you safe from wind, rain, and more.

NATURAL NAVIGATION TECHNIQUES

Ever wonder how you could find your way in the woods without a GPS or smartphone? It's totally possible and really awesome to learn! Using natural navigation means using the world around you to figure out which way you're going and where you are.

HERE ARE SOME BASIC WAYS TO DO THAT:

USING THE SUN

Did you know the sun can help you find your way? It rises in the east and sets in the west. During the day, you can use your watch to help you out. Point the hour hand of your watch at the sun. The line halfway between the hour hand and the 12 o'clock mark on your watch will point south if you're in the Northern Hemisphere. Cool, right?

STAR NAVIGATION

When it's night-time, look up to find the North Star, also known as Polaris, in the Northern Hemisphere. This special star stays almost in the same spot in the sky and always points north. To find it, first spot the Big Dipper constellation. The two stars at the end of the 'cup' part of the Big Dipper point right towards the North Star.

LANDMARKS

You can also use landmarks to help you navigate. Big things like mountains, rivers, or even very tall or unusual trees can help you know where you are. They're like natural signposts telling you which way to go or how to get back to where you started.

SHADOW STICK METHOD

Here's a fun way to use the sun and a stick to find your way!

Stick a straight stick into the ground so it stands up. Mark where the tip of its shadow lands. Wait about 15-30 minutes and mark where the tip of the shadow is again. A line connecting these two marks will show you the direction from west to east in the morning and from east to west in the afternoon.

OBSERVING NATURE

Nature gives us lots of hints about direction if we know where to look. For example, in the Northern Hemisphere, you might find moss growing on the northern side of trees because it likes being cool and moist. Watching where plants grow or how animals behave can give you clues about where you are.

FINDING AND CREATING SHELTER

When you're out exploring, sometimes you need to make a "mini-home" in the woods to keep you safe and warm.

> **Did You Know?**
>
> Long before compasses were around, the Vikings, who were amazing seafarers, had a clever trick to navigate the seas, even on cloudy days. They used something called sunstones! These special stones helped them figure out where the sun was in the sky, so they could sail in the right direction without even seeing the sun.

Here's how you can build a cool fort using stuff you find in nature!

TYPES OF NATURAL SHELTERS

- *Lean-to-Shelter:* This is like making a big tent out of branches. Find a fallen tree or a big branch and lean it against a standing tree. Then, cover it with lots of smaller branches, leaves, or grass to keep the wind and rain out.
- *Debris Hut:* Imagine piling up all your stuffed animals on your bed; that's kind of what a debris hut is like, but with branches and leaves! This snug shelter keeps you warm because it's just the right size.
- *Snow Cave:* If you're in a place with lots of snow, you can dig a cave in the snow. The snow keeps the inside of the cave warm, just like an igloo!

MATERIALS USED FOR MAKING SHELTERS

- Wood: Look for branches and sticks that can help make the walls of your shelter.
- Leaves and Grass: These are great for filling in gaps and keeping the wind out.
- Snow and Ice: If it's winter and snowy, you can use snow to build a cool snow fort.

STEP BY STEP GUIDE TO BUILDING A BASIC LEAN-TO SHELTER

- Find two trees that are close together or one tree with a strong branch.
- Place a long branch across the tree(s) to make the top of your tent.
- Lean smaller branches along this top branch to make the walls.
- Cover everything with lots of leaves and grass to make it cozy.

➢ Make sure the opening of your shelter is away from the wind.

> **Fast Facts**
> Did you know a well-made snow cave can be as warm as a heated room, even if it's really cold outside?

SAFE SHELTER PRACTICES

Making your shelter is super fun, but you have to make sure it's safe too.

Here are some tips to make sure your shelter is the best it can be:

CHOOSING A SAFE SPOT

➢ Stay away from places that could flood (like right next to a river) or where trees might fall.
➢ Pick a spot where you can be seen easily in case you need help.
➢ Don't build too close to water to avoid bugs and stay dry

IMPORTANCE OF STAYING WARM AND DRY

➢ Stuff your shelter with leaves and grass to keep it warm.
➢ Make sure the roof is good at keeping rain out so everything inside stays dry.

If You… don't have lots of branches or leaves, use whatever you can find, like a raincoat or a blanket, to cover your shelter.

FUN ACTIVITY: BUILD YOUR VIRTUAL SHELTER

Now, let's pretend you're in a forest and it's getting dark. You need to build a shelter fast with what you find around you.

- *Scenario:* You find a big stick, some smaller sticks, a bunch of leaves, and you're near a little stream.
- *Challenge:* Use these items to make a shelter that will keep you dry and warm all night.

- **Steps:**
- Choose what kind of shelter you want to build.
- Pick the materials for the walls and the roof.
- Explain why you picked those materials and that type of shelter.

- **Reflection: Think about your shelter:**
- What parts of your shelter do you think are the coolest?
- If you were to build it again, what would you do differently?

This activity will help you think like a true explorer, using what nature gives you to stay safe and snug. Plus, it's a lot of fun to imagine all the different kinds of forts you can build!

Let's put your wilderness knowledge to the test with this fun quiz! See how much you've learned about finding your way and building shelters in the wild.

QUIZ: CAN YOU NAVIGATE AND BUILD LIKE A PRO?

Question 1: Which way does the sun rise and set?

    A. North to south

    B. East towest

    C. West to east

Question 2: What should you do if you need to find your way in the woods without a compass?

    A. Ask a tree for directions

    B. Follow the sound of theriver

    C. Use the sun or stars for direction

Question 3: Which type of natural shelter is made by leaning branches against a tree?

    A. Debris hut

    B. Lean-to shelter

    C. Snowcave

Question 4: What should you do to stay warm in a shelter you built?

    A. Open all the windows

    B. Jump up and down

    C. Use leaves and grass for insulation

Welldone!

You're on your way to becoming a wilderness expert. Keep practicing and exploring, and you'll be a master of the great outdoors in no time!

Chapter 3:

MEET THE FOREST FRIENDS: HOW TO WATCH WILDLIFE SAFELY

When you're out exploring, you might come across all sorts of animals. Some might be tiny like a squirrel, and others might be big like a bear! This chapter will teach you about the animals you might see and how to stay safe around them.

UNDERSTANDING WILDLIFE

Did you know that animals in the wild act very differently from the pets we have at home?

When you're out on an adventure, it's cool to know how these wild animals behave so when you're out on an adventure, it's cool to know how these wild animals behave so you can understand them better and know what to expect.

Let's learn how to be smart and safe around them!

ANIMALS YOU MIGHT SEE

- *Squirrels and Rabbits:* These little critters are super fun to watch as they hop and scurry around. They can be a bit shy, so if you stay quiet and still, you might see them up close!
- *Deer:* Deer are beautiful and might even come close if you're lucky. But remember, it's safest and kindest to watch them from a distance.
- *Bears and Coyotes:* Seeing these is rare, but it's good to remember they might be around. Always respect their space and stay safe.

ANIMAL BEHAVIOURS AND SIGNS

- Tracks: Ever see paw prints in the mud or snow? Those tracks can tell you which animals have been walking on the trail before you. Isn't that like being a detective?
- Noises: Pay attention to the sounds in the wild. Birds chirping happily means all is well, but if they suddenly go quiet, they might be warning of a predator nearby.
- Marks on Trees: Look for scratches or rub marks on trees. Animals like deer and bears leave these marks, which is their way of telling us they've been there.

FAST FACTS

Did you know that when rabbits get scared, they often freeze and stay very still, while squirrels might quickly run up a tree? That's their way of staying safe!

SAFETY MEASURES AND PRECAUTIONS

Seeing wild animals is super exciting, but it's really important to stay safe while exploring.

Here are some tips on what to do if you spot an animal and how to keep your campsite secure from curious creatures.

DO'S AND DON'TS WHEN YOU SEE WILD ANIMALS

- Do: Stay calm, move slowly, and keep a good distance. This keeps both you and the animals safe.
- Don't: Never try to feed them or get too close for a better look. This can scare the animals or make them feel threatened, and they might act defensively.

HOW TO KEEP YOUR CAMPSITE SAFE FROM WILDLIFE

- *Keep it Clean:* Always clean up your campsite and don't leave food or trash out. Wild animals have amazing noses and might come to investigate your leftovers.
- *Store Food Properly:* Use airtight containers to store your food. If you're in an area with bears, hang your food up in a tree to keep it out of reach.
- *Be Scent-Smart:* Remember, even non-food items like toothpaste or lotions can attract animals because they smell interesting. Keep these items sealed up too.

WHAT TO DO IF... SCENARIOS

Adventuring in nature is awesome, but sometimes you might bump into wildlife unexpectedly.

Here's what to do in some common "What if?" situations:

IF YOU BUMP INTO A SNAKE ON YOUR PATH:

Freeze! Stand still and give the snake some time to move away on its own. Remember, snakes usually only strike if they feel threatened or scared.

IF YOU SEE A BEAR:

Talk in a calm voice to let the bear know you're a human and not prey.

Never run away from a bear. Running might make the bear chase you as if you were a game of tag, and bears are very fast!

IF BEES START BUZZING AROUND YOU:

Keep your cool and walk away slowly. Quick movements can make bees think you're a threat, and they might sting

IF YOU GET LOST

The best thing to do if you find yourself lost is to stay exactly where you are. This makes it easier for rescuers to find you. If you have a whistle, blow it three times, pause for a bit, and then blow three times again. Keep repeating this pattern. The sound can really help searchers find you fast.

Do you have a bright hat, scarf, or any other colourful item? Wave it around! This makes you more visible and can catch the attention of someone who is looking for you.

LIFE SAVERS

Always carry a whistle when you're exploring. If you need help, blow three loud blasts on your whistle. This is a universal signal for help and can also scare some animals away.

RESPECT FOR NATURE

Nature is awesome, and we need to take care of it so animals and plants can thrive.

> **Did You Know?**
> Porcupines are really interesting! They can't shoot their quills like arrows, but if you touch them, the quills can stick into your skin. So, it's best to admire these spiky friends from a distance!

WHY WE SHOULD NOT DISTURB WILDLIFE

Watching animals is cool, but getting too close can scare them or even be dangerous. It's best to look at them from a distance and keep quiet.

LEAVE NO TRACE PRINCIPLES

Here are some easy rules to follow when you're outside:

- *Know Before You Go:* Learn about the place you're visiting. Knowing the rules and what to expect helps you protect the environment and have more fun!
- *Pack It In, Pack It Out:* Always take your trash back home with you. Remember, if you brought it, you should bring it back. Nothing should be left behind to spoil the beauty of nature.
- *Keep Nature Natural:* Found a cool rock or a pretty flower? That's awesome! But leave them where you found them so the next visitor can enjoy them too.
- *Share the Space:* The great outdoors is for everyone! Be polite and kind to other explorers. Keep the noise down and let everyone enjoy the peace and beauty of nature.
- *Become a Nature Guardian:* Learn about the animals and plants where you live. You can help nature by doing simple things like planting flowers for bees or picking up trash to keep habitats clean and safe for wildlife.

Let's test your wild animal knowledge with a fun quiz!

INTERACTIVE ACTIVITY: WILDLIFE SAFETY QUIZ

Question 1: What should you do if you see a bear?

    A. Run away fast

    B. Throw food at it to distract it

    C. Speak calmly and back away slowly

Question 2: How can you make sure your campsite doesn't attract animals?

    A. Leave your leftovers outside to keep smells out of your tent

    B. Store food and scented items in airtight containers

    C. Cook very fragrant meals

Question 3: What's a good way to help protect wildlife habitats?

    A. Carve your name into a tree

    B. Follow Leave No Trace principles

    C. Feed wildlife so they get used to humans

This quiz is not only fun but helps you remember how to be safe and respectful while exploring nature. The more you know, the more fun and safe your adventures will be!

Chapter 4:

BE A WILDERNESS DOCTOR: FIRST AID FUN

BASIC FIRST AID SKILLS

When you're adventuring outdoors, sometimes you might get a scrape, cut, or even a bug bite. Don't worry!

Here's how you can take care of these little accidents and keep having fun.

TREATING YOUR CUTS, SCRAPES, AND BRUISES

What to Know: If you scrape your knee or get a cut, that means your skin has opened up a bit. A bruise is what happens when you bump into something hard, but your skin stays closed.

Action Steps to Help You Heal:

1. Clean It: If you get a cut or scrape, the first thing to do is rinse it off with clean, cool water. This helps wash away any dirt or little things that shouldn't be there. You don't even need soap – water does the trick!
2. Stop the Bleeding: Gently press on the wound with a clean cloth or a bandage. Keep pressing until the bleeding stops, which might take a few minutes.
3. Cover It Up: After the bleeding stops, put a clean bandage on it. This keeps out dirt and germs and helps your injuries heal faster without getting infected.

Safety Tips for Injuries: Never touch a wound with dirty hands because it can make it worse by causing an infection. If the cut is deep or if it keeps bleeding and doesn't stop, make sure to tell an adult right away.

INSECT BITES AND STINGS

What to Know: Bugs like mosquitoes, bees, and ants can bite or sting you, and it might hurt or get itchy.

➢ **Action Steps:**
1. Stay Calm: If you get stung, try to walk away from the area calmly. If you run, bees or wasps might chase you and sting more.
2. Remove the Stinger: If a bee stings you and leaves its stinger in your skin, don't pinch it out – this can squeeze more venom into the sting. Instead, gently scrape it out sideways using something like a credit card or your fingernail.
3. Cool It Down: Put something cold like a cold pack or a damp cloth on the sting or bite. This helps make the swelling go down and feel less painful or itchy

➢ **Safety Tips:**

If you get bitten or stung by an insect and start having trouble breathing, feel dizzy, or notice a lot of swelling, it's very important to tell an adult right away. These can be signs of an allergic reaction, and you might need help quickly.

FAST FACTS

Honey Is Super! Not only is honey delicious, but it's also a natural way to fight germs. If you have a small cut or scrape, dabbing a little bit of honey on it can help it heal faster. Just remember, honey is sticky, so cover it with a bandage to keep it clean and avoid getting honey everywhere!

HANDLING SERIOUS EMERGENCIES

Even when you're having lots of fun outdoors, it's important to know how to stay safe in big challenges like extreme cold (that's called hypothermia) or extreme heat (that's called heatstroke)

Here's what you need to know:

1. Hypothermia: This happens when your body gets too cold. You might start shivering a lot and can't stop, feel really tired, get confused, and find it hard to talk properly.

2. Heatstroke: This happens when your body gets too hot. Signs that you might have heatstroke include having a very high body temperature, skin that feels hot and looks red and dry, feeling confused, having a throbbing headache, and feeling dizzy.

WHAT TO DO IF YOU THINK YOU HAVE HYPOTHERMIA?

- Get Warm: First, try to get to a warmer place right away. This could be inside a tent or under lots of blankets to help warm up your body.
- Dry Clothes: If your clothes are wet, they can make you even colder. Change into dry clothing if you have some.
- Huddle Up: If you're not alone, staying close to others can help too. Sharing body warmth by huddling close together can make everyone feel warmer.

STAYING HEALTHY OUTDOORS

Having fun outside is awesome, but it's also important to keep yourself healthy and strong while you're exploring. This part of the chapter will show you how to stay hydrated, avoid getting sick, and keep your energy up during your adventures.

HYDRATION IS KEY

➢ What to Know: Your body needs lots of water to work right, especially when you're running around and playing. If you don't drink enough water, you can get dehydrated, which isn't good when you're exploring or having fun outside.

ACTION STEPS:

1. Carry Water: Always bring more water than you think you'll need. It's much better to have extra water than to run out.

2. Drink Regularly: Don't just wait until you feel thirsty to drink water. Make a plan to take a few sips every 30 minutes, even if you're not thirsty yet.

3. Check Your Pee: Yep, you read that right! Checking the color of your pee can help you know if you're drinking enough water. If it's light yellow, you're doing great. If it's dark, you need to drink more water.

EATING RIGHT IN THE WILD

➢ What to Know: Choosing good foods to eat while you're outdoors helps you have the energy to explore and have fun all day.

Action Steps:

Pack Smart Snacks: Bring snacks that are easy to carry and good for you, like nuts, dried fruits, and granola bars. These snacks don't take up much space and give you a big energy boost!

Plan Your Meals: Think ahead about what you'll eat and when during your trip. This helps you make sure you have enough energy all day long.

KEEPING CLEAN

Staying clean is key not just to feeling good, but also to staying healthy while you're enjoying the outdoors.

➢ What to Know: Being clean is important because it helps keep you from getting sick.

Action Steps:

Hand Washing: Always wash your hands with soap and water before you eat anything and after you go to the bathroom. This is one of the best ways to stay healthy.

Stay Tidy: Keep your camping area clean to stop animals and bugs from being attracted to your site. Plus, a clean campsite is a nice place to come back to after a day of adventures!

INTERACTIVE ACTIVITY: FIRST AID SIMULATION

Get ready to put your new first aid skills into action with a super fun role-play activity! You'll pretend to handle different health scenarios that could happen while you're exploring outdoors.

Let's see how you can help and what you've learned!

ACTIVITY SETUP

Materials Needed: Grab some bandages, clean clothes, a pretend first aid kit, and some scenario cards.

HOW IT WORKS

Draw a Card: Start by picking a scenario that describes a health situation you might face, like a sprained ankle or a bee sting, and then draw that on a piece of paper.

Act It Out: Choose one friend to be the patient and another to be the first aider. The first aider will use their first aid knowledge to help the patient, just like in a real emergency.

Review: After you are done with the scenario, talk about what you and your friends did well and what you all could do better next time. This helps everyone learn!

LEARNING OBJECTIVES

- **Practice Makes Perfect:** By practising, you'll learn how to handle common injuries safely and effectively. This is super important for keeping everyone safe during adventures.
- **Think Fast:** You'll also get better at quick thinking and solving problems, which is really useful in emergency situations.

STAYING HEALTHY AND HAPPY

Staying healthy is all about making sure you don't get sick so you can keep playing and having fun outside.

Here are some tips on how to stay safe and feel great:

AVOIDING BUG BITES

➢ **What to Know:**
Bites from little bugs like ticks and mosquitoes can make you feel really sick, so it's super important to keep them away.

➢ **What You Can Do:**
Use Bug Spray: Spray on some bug repellent that's safe for kids. Remember to put more on if you've been swimming or sweating.
Dress Smart: Wear long sleeves and pants to keep those pesky bugs off your skin.

SAFE EATING PRACTICES

➢ **What to Know:**
Eating bad food or drinking yucky water can make your tummy really upset.

➢ **What you can do:**
1. Check Your Food: Always make sure your food is cooked the right way and kept cool and dry.
2. Purify Water: If you're not sure if the water is clean, use special water-cleaning tablets or a filter to make it safe to drink.

WHAT TO DO IF YOU THINK YOU ATE SOMETHING BAD?
Quick Tips:
1. Stay Calm: Don't worry, just stay calm and find an adult to help you.
2. Tell Someone About Your Food: Let someone know what you ate that might have made you feel sick. This can help figure out how to make you feel better.
3. Drink Water: Keep drinking plenty of clean water to help your body get rid of the yuckiness.

QUIZ: FIRST AID AND STAYING HEALTHY OUTDOORS

Instructions: Choose the best answer for each question. Good luck, and have fun!

Question 1: What should you do first if you get a scrape while hiking?

A. Ignore it, it will go away.

B. Cover it with leaves.

C. Wash it with clean water

Question 2: Why is it important to drink water when you're playing outside?

A. It makes you run faster.

B. It keeps your body healthy and prevents dehydration.

C. It tastes good

Question 3: What is the best thing to do if you see a bug on your friend's back?

A. Scream and run away.

B. Ignore it; it's just a bug.

C. Tell your friend calmly and help them brush it off safely

Question 4: If you are helping someone who feels very cold and is shivering, what should you do?

> A. Move them to a warmer place and wrap them in a blanket.
> B. Give them a cold drink.
> C. Ask them to jump around to warm up.

Question 5: How can you check if you are drinking enough water while playing outdoors?

> A. Check the color of your pee. If it's light yellow, you're hydrated.
> B. Check if you are sweating.
> C. See how thirsty you are.

Question 6: What should you use to remove a bee stinger?

> A. Pull it out with your fingers.
> B. Scrape it out sideways with a credit card or your fingernail.
> C. Bite it out

Question 7: What is one thing you should always do after treating a wound?

> A. Put mud on it to keep it cool.
> B. Show it to everyone.
> C. Cover it with a bandage.

Chapter 5:

CRAFTY IN THE WILD: MAKING TOOLS AND FIRE

FORAGING FUN: FINDING FOOD IN NATURE

Foraging for food in the wild is like going on a treasure hunt in nature where you can discover some yummy snacks!

But remember, not all treasures are good to eat. Always have a grown-up guide who knows which snacks are safe and which ones to leave behind. This way, you can enjoy your adventure without any oopsies. It's always super important to know how to do it safely so you stay healthy and happy.

Here's how you can find tasty treats in nature without any worries:

SAFE PLANTS AND INSECTS TO EAT

What to Know: Not all plants and bugs are good to eat. Some might look nice but can actually make you feel really sick. It's very important to know which ones are okay to munch on.

➢ **Action Steps:**

1. Learn About Safe Plants: Before you head out, learn about which plants are safe to eat. Be sure to do this with an adult that knows what is safe to eat! Look for things like berries, nuts, and some special leaves that you can eat.

2. Spot Edible Bugs: Did you know that in many parts of the world, eating bugs is normal because they're packed with protein and nutrients like omega 3s? Yummy bugs like ants,

crickets and grasshoppers are not only safe but nutritious. Remember, always cook them first because they can carry tiny worms that you can't see.

3. Bring a Guide: Take along a guidebook or use a mobile app that helps you know which plants and insects are safe to eat. This way, you can be sure about what you're picking.

LEARNING TO HARVEST: HOW TO BE A NATURE-FRIENDLY FORAGER

What to Know: Harvesting correctly helps protect plants and makes sure there's more food for later.

➤ **Action Steps:**

1. Gentle Picking: Be gentle when you pick plants. This helps them stay healthy and keep growing.

2. Take What You Need: Only take what you'll actually eat. This means no food goes to waste, and there's plenty left for animals and other people who might be foraging.

BEWARE OF LOOK-ALIKES

➤ **What to Know:** Some plants look like they are safe to eat but are actually poisonous. This can be very dangerous.

➤ **Action Steps:**

1. Double-Check: Always make sure you know exactly what a plant or bug is before you eat it. Use a guidebook or an app to help you.

2. When in Doubt, Leave It Out: If you're not sure if something is safe to eat, it's best to leave it alone.

FAST FACTS

Did you know that every part of a dandelion is edible? From the roots to the flowers, you can eat them in salads, make tea, and much more!

THE BASICS OF HUNTING AND FISHING

Hunting and fishing aren't just ways to find food, they're also ancient skills that connect you with nature and teach valuable life lessons.

SIMPLE TRAPS FOR SMALL ANIMALS

- ➢ What to Know: Trapping is a way to catch small animals without needing to chase them. It's like setting up a little surprise that works while you're doing other things.

- ➢ **Action Steps:**

1. Learn to Make a Snare: A snare is a loop made of wire or strong string. When an animal like a rabbit walks through it, the loop tightens around it gently.

2. Set Traps in the Right Places: Put your snares in spots where small animals are likely to go, like little paths they use or near their homes called burrows.

FISHING IS FUN WITH JUST A FEW THINGS!

➢ **What to Know:** You don't need lots of fancy equipment to catch fish.

➢ **Action Steps:**

1. Early Bird Catches the Worm: Waking up early is great for fishing! People who start their day early are often more alert and healthy.

2. Make Your Own Fishing Rod: All you need is a long stick, some string, and a hook! Making and using your own fishing rod can teach you how to be patient and careful – skills that are good for lots of things in life.

3. Tying Knots: Learn how to tie a hook to your string so it stays put when you catch a big one.

4. Pick the Perfect Spot: Try to fish near rocks or plants. These are places where fish like to hang out because they feel safe and find food there

5. Catch and Let Go: Sometimes, we put the fish back after we catch them. This helps us learn to take care of nature and keep fish numbers healthy for the future. It's a great way to learn about ecosystems, where fish live, and why they are important to our world.

ETHICAL HUNTING AND FISHING: CARING FOR NATURE

What to Know: Being kind to nature and only taking what you need is part of being a good outdoorsman.

➢ **Action Steps:**

1. **Follow Local Rules:** Always stick to the rules about hunting and fishing in your area.
2. **Respect Wildlife:** Make sure your fishing and hunting doesn't hurt the environment or animal numbers. Fish wisely by getting a fishing licence, knowing the types of fish, and following all the rules about fishing and boating.
3. **Prevent Harm:** Keep harmful plants and animals out of the water. Learn about protecting our waters and be careful not to spread unwanted species
4. **Keep Learning:** Grow your fishing skills and share your tips with others, especially kids. It's fun to see others enjoy fishing with your help.
5. **Be Nice to Nature:** Take care of the places you fish and hunt. Don't leave trash behind, and be careful not to pollute the land and water. Always ask if it's okay to fish on someone else's land.
6. **Be Polite:** Give other anglers space and try not to disturb their fishing fun. If it's crowded, maybe find a quieter spot to enjoy.
7. **Select What You Keep:** Sometimes, it's best to let the really big or small fish go and only keep fish that are just the right size. This helps keep the fish population healthy.
8. **Preserve Your Passion:** Lead by example and teach others about respectful fishing. Focus on the fun and the adventure, not just the size and number of fish.

> *Did You Know?*
> For thousands of years, people have used simple tools like spears and nets for fishing, proving that you don't need fancy equipment to be successful!

ADVENTURE CRAFTING IN THE WOODS: BECOME A NATURE DETECTIVE AND INVENTOR!

➢ **What to Know:** The woods are like a treasure chest filled with stuff to make your very own tools – like sticks, stones, and vines!

➢ **Action Steps:**

1. Scavenger Hunt: Start your adventure by searching for strong sticks, smooth stones, and long vines around you.

2. Choose Your Creation: Think about what you want to build. It could be a fishing rod to pretend to fish or a small scoop for digging.

3. Build It: Use vines to tie stones to sticks to make a pretend hammer, or attach a sharp stone to a stick to create a spear for pretend adventures.

FUN SIMPLE TOOLS TO MAKE:

➢ **Fishing Net:** Use vines and sticks to weave your own fishing net. It's a handy tool to catch fish for a fresh meal in the wild.

➢ **Leafy Basket:** Pick some big, bendy leaves and weave them into a basket. It's perfect for holding all the cool stuff you find, like pretty stones or yummy berries!

➢ **Rockin' Hammer:** Find a strong stick and a smooth rock. Tie them together to make your own hammer. You can use it to crack open nuts or help build a cool fort!

➢ **Nature's Cup:** Spot a big leaf or find a piece of bark shaped like a bowl. Use it to scoop up water from a stream, or catch raindrops to drink like a jungle explorer!

➢ **Shadow Compass:** Find a straight stick and place it upright in the ground. Use its shadow to help you figure out directions and find your way through the wilderness.

➢ SAFETY TIPS

Always make sure to have an adult around when you're making your tools, especially if you're using sharp stones or big sticks. They can help make sure everything is safe and fun!

INTERACTIVE ACTIVITY: CREATE YOUR SURVIVAL TOOL

Let's put on our inventor hats! You're going to make a super cool tool using things you find outside.

WHAT YOU'LL NEED

Gather up some sticks, stones, leaves, and vines from outside.

HOW TO MAKE YOUR SURVIVAL TOOL?

- ➢ **Dream It Up:** Think about an awesome tool you'd need for an adventure. What special job would it do?
- ➢ **Create It:** Use the sticks, stones, leaves, and vines you found to build your tool. You might make something to hold treasures or a tool to write secret messages in the dirt!
- ➢ **Test It Out:** Try using your tool. Can it scoop up small stones? Can it help you collect leaves without using your hands?

WHAT YOU'LL LEARN:

- ➤ Use Your Imagination: Think creatively to solve problems and invent something cool.
- ➤ Discover Materials: Learn how different natural materials can work together to make something amazing.

FIRE-MAKING TECHNIQUES :

In the wild, being able to start a fire is super important! Fire gives us warmth, and light, and helps us cook food and make water safe to drink.

- ➤ **What to Know:** There are many ways to start a fire, but you should always have an adult help you.
- ➤ **Action Steps:**
1. **Watch and Learn:** Observe how an adult can use just a tiny spark to start a fire safely.
2. **Helping Hands:** You can collect small twigs and dry leaves to help prepare.
3. **The Hand Drill:** Twist a stick really fast between your palms over some dry wood. This creates heat from friction that can start a fire. It needs patience and strong hands!
4. **The Bow Drill:** Like the hand drill, but you use a bow to spin the stick faster. This makes it a bit easier to create the needed heat.
5. **The Fire Plow:** Push a stick quickly back and forth on a flat piece of wood. This heats up tiny wood pieces until they glow and start a fire.

6. **Rocks and Sparks:** Find two different rocks, one harder than the other. Strike the sharp edge of the harder rock against the softer one to create sparks. Catch these sparks on something super dry to start your fire.

7. **Sunlight Lens:** On a sunny day, you can make a tiny fire using just the sun! Find a clear piece of ice or a glass lens like from a magnifying glass or eyeglasses. Shape the ice into a circle or use the glass to catch the sun's rays. Point it at dry leaves or twigs and watch the magic happen as they start to smoke and create a little fire! Always have a grown-up help you with this sunny science trick!

SAFETY FIRST WHILE HANDLING FIRE

Fire is super useful but also something that needs to be treated with respect and care.

- Clear the Area: Before starting a fire, make sure the area is free from leaves, twigs, or anything that could catch fire accidentally.
- Stay Close: Always stick with an adult when you're near a fire to stay safe and learn the right way to handle fire.

If You… want to make a signal for help, you can learn to add some green leaves to create smoke, but remember, only with an adult's help.

QUIZ: IMPORTANT SURVIVAL TECHNIQUES:

Instructions: Choose the best answer for each question to test your survival skills. Have fun exploring your knowledge!

Question 1: What should you always do before you eat a plant you found in the wild?

    A. Eat it right away if it looks good.
    B. Make sure it is safe by checking with an adult or a guidebook.
    C. Feed it to your pet first

Question 2: If you want to make a simple fishing rod, what materials would you need from nature?

    A. A plastic bottle, some string, and a rubber band.
    B. A rock, some mud, and leaves.
    C. A long stick, some strong string, and a hook

Question 3: Which of these insects is safe to eat if cooked properly?

    A. Maggots
    B. Spiders
    C. Grasshoppers

Question 4: What is the best place to set up a snare for catching small animals?

    A. On a narrow path where animals commonly walk.
    B. In the middle of a large open field.
    C. In a tree.

Question 5: What can you use to start a fire using the power of the sun?

    A. A flashlight

    B. A magnifying glass

    C. A piece of ice

Question 6: Why is it important to use natural resources responsibly when making tools?

    A. Because it makes the tools look nicer.

    B. So there is enough for others and to keep nature healthy.

    C. It isn't important; nature has plenty

Question 7: If you need to signal for help using a fire, what can you add to make more smoke?

    A. Green leaves or branches

    B. Dry leaves

    C. Flowers

Final Words

Way to go, awesome explorer!

You've raced through this wilderness adventure guide like a pro, uncovering all the basics of survival and learning how to be a fantastic outdoor adventurer. You've filled your adventure backpack, navigated twisty trails, and even made some awesome tools with your own hands. All these new skills are sure to make your outdoor adventures safe and super exciting.

Remember, all the cool survival skills you've read about in this book aren't just for looking at – they're for doing! Whether you're building a fort in your backyard, going on a hike with your family, or imagining adventures in the wild, these skills are your trusty tools for any adventure you dream up.

You've become an expert at being ready for anything. You know how to stay safe, help your friends, and take good care of nature. Every time you pack your adventure bag or tie a knot, you're putting what you've learned into action, making every adventure an amazing one.

The end of this book isn't the end of your adventures – it's just the beginning! You've learned so many cool things, and here's how you can keep growing and having fun with your new skills:

- **Practice Makes Perfect:** Use every opportunity to practise your new skills. Tie knots on a rainy day or help plan your family's next camping trip. The more you practise, the better you'll get.

A COMPLETE KID'S GUIDE TO WILDERNESS SURVIVAL

- **Stay Curious:** There's so much to learn about the plants, animals, and places around you. Why not start a nature journal? You can write down and draw all the amazing things you find. It's like being a nature detective
- **Teach Others:** Share your awesome survival skills with friends and family. Teaching others is a super way to understand things even better yourself, and you'll learn even more as you explain what you know.

Always remember – adventure wisely.

➢ Always tell someone where you're going, like a family member or a friend.

➢ Stick to paths you know are safe, and never go exploring alone.

➢ Use your survival skills to make smart decisions, and always take your essential gear with you.

You're now a **Guardian of Nature**.

By learning all these amazing survival skills, you're not just getting really good at handling yourself in the wild – you're also learning to take care of our Earth. Every tree you climb, stream you jump over, bird you spot, and bug you find is part of a huge, wonderful world called an ecosystem. And guess what? Now you're a part of that big, beautiful world too!

Imagine all the awesome adventures that are waiting for you. There are tall mountains that challenge you to climb higher, mysterious forests full of secrets to uncover, and countless trails that invite you to explore. Each time you step outside for an adventure, you'll face new challenges. But with your skills and bravery, you're all set to tackle them!

So lace up your boots, pack your gear, and step into your next adventure with confidence

The wild is calling – *are you ready to answer?*

Wilderness Whiz: The Answer Key to Your Outdoor Quizzes

Chapter 1 :

➢ True or False

False – For a day trip, something small like a lightweight emergency shelter or space blanket is just fine.

True – It's always a good idea to be able to make water safe to drink if you need to.

➢ Quiz Answers

Correct Answer: C – Your plans and where you're going.
Correct Answer: B – A flashlight and extra batteries.
Correct Answer: A – Layers help you stay comfy and safe as the weather changes.
Correct Answer: B – Carry a map and a compass.

Chapter 2:

➢ Quiz Answers

Correct Answer: B – The sun rises in the east and sets in the west.

Correct Answer: C – The sun and stars can help you figure out which way is which.

Correct Answer: B – A lean-to shelter is like making a tent with branches and a tree.

Correct Answer: C – Leaves and grass can help keep your shelter warm.

Chapter 3

Quiz Answers

Correct Answer: C – Speak calmly and back away slowly

Correct Answer: B – Store food and scented items in airtight containers

Correct Answer: B – Follow Leave No Trace principles

Chapter 4

Quiz Answers

Correct Answer: C) Wash it with clean water

Correct Answer: B) It keeps your body healthy and prevents dehydration

Correct Answer: C) Tell your friend calmly and help them brush it off safely

Correct Answer: A) Move them to a warmer place and wrap them in a blanket

Correct Answer: A) Check the colour of your pee. If it's light yellow, you're hydrated

Correct Answer: B) Scrape it out sideways with a credit card or your fingernail

Correct Answer: C) Cover it with a bandage

Chapter 5

Quiz Answers

Correct Answer: B) Make sure it is safe by checking with an adult or a guidebook

Correct Answer: C) A long stick, some strong string, and a hook.

Correct Answer: C) Grasshoppers

Correct Answer: A) On a narrow path where animals commonly walk

Correct Answer: B) A magnifying glass

Correct Answer: B) So there is enough for others and to keep nature healthy

Correct Answer: A) Green leaves or branches

Dear Adventurer,

Thank you for purchasing "A Complete Kid's Guide to Wilderness Survival." Your support means the world to us! We hope this book inspires and empowers you to explore the great outdoors with confidence and curiosity.

We would love to hear about your experience with the book. If you enjoyed it, please consider leaving a review on Amazon. Your feedback helps us improve and reach more budding adventurers like you.

Happy adventuring!

Warm regards,

A. Cox